Cornerstones of Freedom

The Declaration of Independence

R. Conrad Stein

CHILDRENS PRESS®
CHICAGO

Library of Congress Cataloging-in-Publication Data

Stein, R. Conrad.
The Declaration of Independence / by R. Conrad Stein.
p. cm. – (Cornerstones of freedom)
ISBN 0-516-46693-3
1. United States. Declaration of Independence—Juvenile literature. 2. United States—Politics and government—1775–1783—Juvenile literature. [1. United States. Declaration of Independence. 2. United States—Politics and government—1775–1783.] I. Title. II. Series.
E221.S74 1995
973.3'13—dc20 94-24370
CIP
AC

Printed in China
16 17 18 19 20 R 13 12 11 62

It was a rainy, forbidding night in July 1776 when Caesar Rodney of the Delaware Colony received an urgent message: COME AT ONCE. YOUR VOTE IS URGENTLY NEEDED. Rodney saddled his horse and began a treacherous, eighty-mile ride to Philadelphia. Caesar Rodney headed to Philadelphia for the most important decision of his life: to vote yes or no for independence.

Caesar Rodney was called to Philadelphia (below), which was the capital of the American colonies in the 1770s.

For 150 years, the British Empire had established colonies on the eastern shores of what is now the United States. By the mid-1700s, the thirteen colonies held 2.5 million people. The colonists were prosperous, and for most of their history, British leaders allowed them to run their own affairs. In 1763, Britain ended more than seventy years of war with France in North America, the last stage being the French and Indian War (1754-1763). It had been an expensive war to conduct, and the king of England now needed money to continue running his empire. The king turned to the

British troops march through the streets of Boston.

New Yorkers protest the Stamp Act (left), a British law that required colonists to pay taxes on legal stamps such as those pictured below.

American colonies and imposed taxes on them. The British taxed tea and legal notes called stamps. These measures enraged the American colonists because they had no representatives in the British Parliament to vote against the new taxes. Other heavy-handed actions such as the stationing of troops in colonial cities caused bitter anti-British feelings to sweep America. A minority of colonists began to utter a word with explosive potential. That word—*Revolution!*—spread across the American wilderness, growing from a whisper to a thunderclap.

The Battle of Lexington

Ragtag colonial armies began waging an undeclared war against British troops in April 1775. After major battles at Lexington and Concord, Massachusetts, the Second Continental Congress was assembled hastily on May 10, 1775. (The First Continental Congress had met in 1774.) Caesar Rodney, a soldier with the Delaware Militia, was a delegate to the Second Congress. The delegates met in Philadelphia and decided to establish a Continental Army to fight the British. The Congress was also debating whether they should make the most dramatic vote thus far in American history: independence from Great Britain—yes or no.

By the summer of 1776, the colonies were in an all-out war with their mother country, England. The road to Philadelphia took Rodney past lonely farms and cut through untamed woods. He was forty-eight years old and weakened by a prolonged illness. Still, he urged on his horse and forged toward Philadelphia, where he knew he would witness history. It was mid-afternoon of the following day when he galloped up to Philadelphia's State House (later named Independence Hall). Without removing his spurs or brushing the mud off his clothes, Rodney took his seat with the Delaware delegation. The voting process had already begun. When the question of independence—aye or nay—was posed to Delaware, Rodney shouted out, "Aye!"

Caesar Rodney

The British battle the Americans at Concord, Massachusetts.

The Delaware vote helped to sway other delegations. By the end of the session, twelve of the thirteen English colonies had chosen to walk the dangerous path of independence. Only New York, whose delegates were locked in arguments, failed to vote. The date of this historic meeting was July 2, 1776. Some historians believe the second of July ought to be celebrated as American Independence Day. But at another meeting held two days later, the delegates approved the most famous document in American history, the Declaration of Independence. Like a trumpet blast, the

The Philadelphia State House, where the Second Continental Congress met. Today, this historic building is called Independence Hall.

The Second Continental Congress meets.

Declaration told the world that a new nation had been born.

In the months leading up to this historic event, Americans had divided into roughly three opinion groups: one-third favored independence; one-third wanted reconciliation with England; and still another third were fence-sitters, undecided about a course of action. Caesar Rodney's Delaware delegation was a good example. Of the three Delaware representatives, Rodney supported independence, another man opposed it, and a third made up his mind only after Rodney's dramatic entrance into the hall.

The colonists' hesitancy to declare independence was understandable. England was the most powerful country in the world. Never before had a British colony broken away from the mother country. Writing the Declaration of Independence was the same as drafting a declaration of war. If the war were lost, those who had signed the independence document would likely be hung for treason by vengeful English leaders.

These dire consequences mattered little to American radicals—those colonists who urged independence at any price. The radicals argued that the fighting had already begun. Now it was only right and proper to prepare a formal paper recognizing a state of war with England and telling the world that America was free from British rule. In June 1776, Congress had decided that it would write this declaration.

The task of writing the document was given to a committee of five men. Three of these five would grow to be some of the most revered names in American history: Benjamin Franklin, John Adams, and Thomas Jefferson. The other two authors were Roger Sherman of Connecticut and Robert Livingston of New York.

At seventy years of age, Benjamin Franklin was the oldest signer of the Declaration. His countrymen hailed him as a scientist, scholar, inventor, and a wise political adviser. He had chosen the path of independence only two

Benjamin Franklin, one of the most respected and influential Americans of the colonial era

years earlier. Franklin's son, William, remained loyal to Britain, and political arguments between the father and son split the family. Benjamin Franklin was considerably depressed over the situation, but he remained on the side of independence.

John Adams played a key role in drafting the Declaration of Independence. He went on to be the nation's first vice president under George Washington. He was then elected president and served from 1797 to 1801.

John Adams, from Massachusetts, was a radical who had dedicated his life to the cause. Adams was fearless in debate and often made bitter enemies of those colonists who were fence-sitters or who were still loyal to England.

Thomas Jefferson was the man who actually wrote the document. The committee realized that a document written by five different men might be difficult to understand. Hoping to produce a convincing document, the committee gave Jefferson the task. John Adams told Jefferson there were three important reasons why Jefferson should do the writing: "Reason first—you are a Virginian, and a Virginian ought to appear at the head of this business. Reason second—I am obnoxious, suspected, and unpopular. You are very much otherwise. Reason third—you can write ten times better than I can."

Jefferson was more than just a gifted writer. He was a genius in many fields, the type of glorious star who rises only once in a generation. The thirty-three-year-old Jefferson was one of the youngest members of Congress, yet he could read, write, and speak four foreign languages: Greek, Latin, French, and Italian. He designed buildings, composed music, and experimented in science. A voracious reader, he pored through all of the major classics while he was still in his teens.

For most of his life, Jefferson had been a loyal

Thomas Jefferson (right) wrote the Declaration of Independence in the Philadelphia house pictured below. Jefferson went on to become the governor of Virginia in 1779, served as vice president under John Adams, and was the third president of the United States (1801–1809).

subject of England. He once wrote, "There is not in the British Empire a man who more cordially loves a union with Great Britain than I do." But by 1776, even Jefferson was convinced that separation from Great Britain was the only course open to the colonies.

Jefferson wrote the Declaration of Independence on the second floor of a house at Seventh and Market Streets in Philadelphia. He was renting the house from a bricklayer named Jacob Graff. Jefferson worked standing up, not sitting down, at a writing table that is still preserved. He kept long hours, sometimes writing well past midnight. He wrote with the point of a goose quill dipped in ink. It was the common pen of the time, but it was a devilish instrument to use. It scratched, it smeared, and it held so little ink it had to be dipped in the inkwell following every word.

Jefferson used this portable writing desk (above), and wrote with a quill pen like the one pictured below. The silver inkwell pictured here was used in the signing of the Declaration of Independence as well as the Constitution in 1787.

To break his tiresome routine, Jefferson took long walks. He was an athletic man who stood six-feet, two-inches tall in an age when the average man's height was five-feet, five-inches.

Sometimes John Adams or the aging Ben Franklin accompanied Jefferson on his hikes, but they were unable to keep up with the taller man's brisk pace. His walks took him to the countryside or to Philadelphia's waterfront, where ships crowded at the docks. All the time, his head buzzed with thoughts of the project—words to add here, sentences to change there.

Thomas Jefferson

Thomas Jefferson began the Declaration with words that have thrilled students of history for more than two hundred years:

When in the Course of human events, it becomes necessary for one people to dissolve the political bands which have connected them with another, and to assume among the powers of the earth, the separate and equal station to which the Laws of Nature and of Nature's God entitle them, a decent respect to the opinions of mankind requires that they should declare the causes which impel them to the separation.

In the first half of this powerful sentence, Jefferson announced that the colonies had separated from England. In the second half of the same sentence, he promised to state the reasons, or the "truths," behind the decision to separate.

He continued:

We hold these truths to be self-evident, that all men are created equal, that they are endowed by their Creator with certain unalienable Rights, that among these are Life, Liberty and the pursuit of Happiness. That to secure these rights, Governments are instituted among Men, deriving their just powers from the consent of the governed. . . .

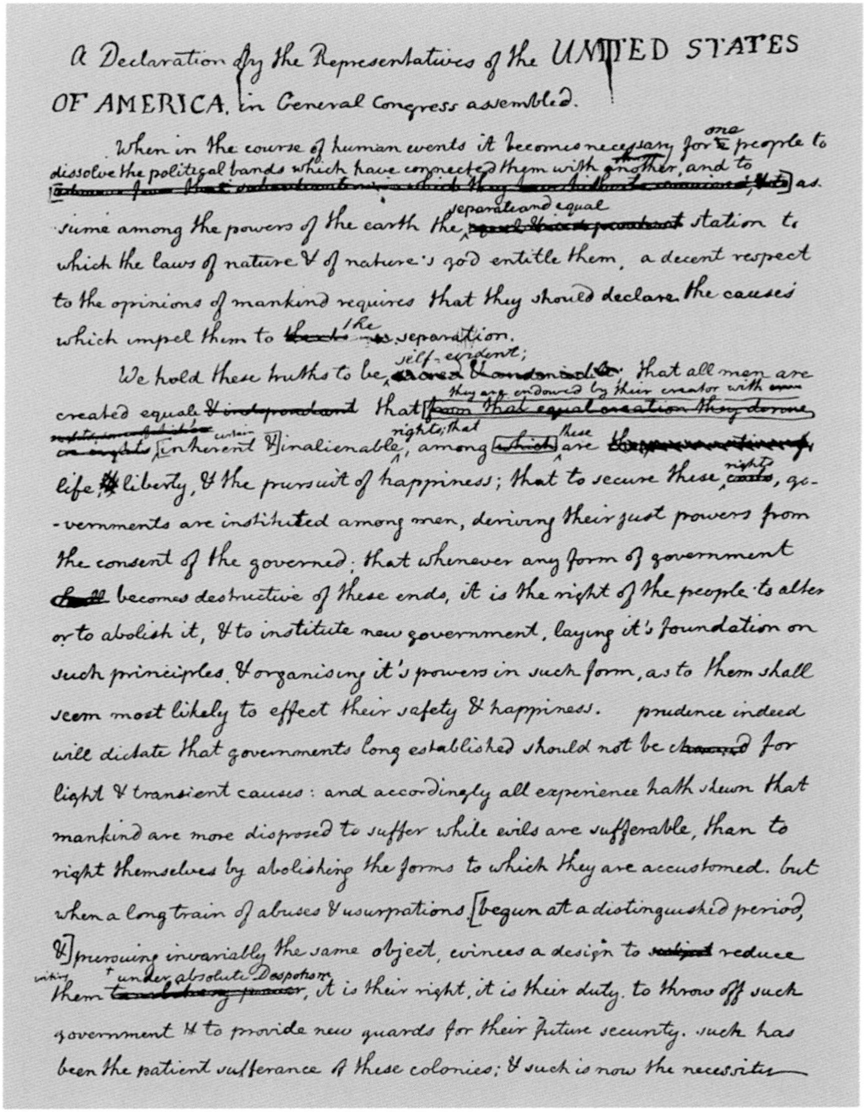

A Declaration by the Representatives of the UNITED STATES OF AMERICA, in General Congress assembled.

When in the course of human events it becomes necessary for one people to dissolve the political bands which have connected them with another, and to assume among the powers of the earth the separate and equal station to which the laws of nature & of nature's god entitle them, a decent respect to the opinions of mankind requires that they should declare the causes which impel them to the separation.

We hold these truths to be self-evident; that all men are created equal; that they are endowed by their creator with certain inherent & inalienable rights; that among these are life, liberty, & the pursuit of happiness; that to secure these rights, governments are instituted among men, deriving their just powers from the consent of the governed; that whenever any form of government becomes destructive of these ends, it is the right of the people to alter or to abolish it, & to institute new government, laying it's foundation on such principles & organising it's powers in such form, as to them shall seem most likely to effect their safety & happiness. prudence indeed will dictate that governments long established should not be changed for light & transient causes: and accordingly all experience hath shewn that mankind are more disposed to suffer while evils are sufferable, than to right themselves by abolishing the forms to which they are accustomed. but when a long train of abuses & usurpations [begun at a distinguished period, &] pursuing invariably the same object, evinces a design to reduce them under absolute Despotism, it is their right, it is their duty, to throw off such government & to provide new guards for their future security. such has been the patient sufferance of these colonies; & such is now the necessity

Jefferson's handwritten draft of the opening section of the Declaration of Independence

These celebrated words state the belief that the king and the common person are equal in the eyes of God. Therefore, governments can exist only with the consent of the people they govern. This was an idea that was born in England and was nurtured in the frontier of America.

The next clause contained the Declaration's real fire:

That whenever any Form of Government becomes destructive of these ends, it is the Right of the People to alter and abolish it. . . .

This right of a people to "alter or abolish" a government was a revolutionary concept. It would shake the earth for centuries.

The Declaration of Independence laid out the reasons why the Americans were rebelling against England. According to British thinking, this American rebellion violated the law. Jefferson forcefully rejected this idea—he

Franklin, Jefferson, Adams, Livingston, and Sherman (left to right) debate the Declaration.

explained that the Americans were justified in their actions. He claimed that the British treatment of the colonies was itself a breach of the law. But to what law did Jefferson refer? Certainly not the laws in the colonial statute books, most of which were written by British lawmakers. Instead, Jefferson cited a higher law, a natural law—"the Laws of Nature and of Nature's God."

The philosopher John Locke

The belief in a natural law, one more powerful even than the decrees of a king, had been developed by British and French philosophers more than one hundred years earlier. John Locke was a prominent British philosopher who lived in the 1600s. Locke argued that God created divine laws at the dawn of time. People naturally obey these laws as they pursue liberty and happiness. When kings and governments set up laws that interfere with this natural pursuit, they—the rulers—disrupt divine law.

In a letter written in 1823, Jefferson looked back and claimed the words of the Declaration came purely from his own heart. "I turned to neither book nor pamphlet when writing it," he said. But Jefferson's mind was a storehouse of ideas. He had read Locke, as he had read all of the important philosophers. Today, most scholars conclude the democratic ideas of Locke are wondrously expressed in Jefferson's Declaration of Independence.

The longest section of the Declaration lists twenty-seven grievances the American colonists claimed against the British government. Jefferson's main complaints had to do with the king's taxes on Americans and the presence of British troops in the colonies.

After the list of grievances, Jefferson wrote a strong statement of independence: ". . . That these United Colonies are, and of Right ought to be Free and Independent States . . ." And the very last sentence of the Declaration was intended to rally the delegates into a firm and unwavering stand for revolution: "And for the support of this declaration . . . we mutually pledge to each other our Lives, our Fortunes and our sacred Honor."

It took Jefferson seventeen days to write the Declaration of Independence. Occasionally, he showed samples of the unfinished manuscript to John Adams and Benjamin Franklin. In an early version, Jefferson had written, "We hold these Truths to be sacred and undeniable, that all men are created equal . . ." Franklin saw this, crossed out "sacred and undeniable," and inserted the now-famous phrase "self-evident." Franklin thought the change would make the writing stronger, and scholars today agree he was correct. Jefferson also laboriously rewrote many of his own passages.

On July 2, 1776, the same day Congress voted

Jefferson (right) discusses a passage of the Declaration with Benjamin Franklin (left).

for independence, the membership began debating the merits of Jefferson's Declaration. Delegates bickered with each other, and many changes were made to the exact wording Jefferson had worked so hard to perfect. Jefferson later called these changes "mutilations."

Most of the arguments were minor, but one paragraph severely divided the membership. This paragraph dealt with slavery. Included in

Jefferson's list of grievances against the king was a long, angry argument against slavery. Jefferson equated the slave trade with the work of evil pirates, and he denounced the idea of slavery as an "assemblage of horrors." It is curious that Jefferson would blame the British king for slavery since the colonists, themselves, held about half a million slaves. These slaves did not work for King George III, but rather for the profit of their American masters. Even Jefferson, who claimed to despise slavery, owned 150 slaves, who worked on his Virginia plantation.

Jefferson's denouncement of slavery disturbed the delegates from the South, where plantation owners relied on slaves to work their fields. At the urging of South Carolina and Georgia, the antislavery paragraph was excluded from the Declaration. As glorious as the document was, the phrase "all men are created equal" remained somewhat empty. It certainly did not apply to the thousands of slaves in the American colonies.

After two days of debate, the Declaration of Independence was approved by Congress on July 4, 1776. It was, in effect, the birth certificate of the United States of America. Congress decided that an official copy of the Declaration should be printed in ornamental script on parchment paper. After this copy was completed, the actual signing of the document

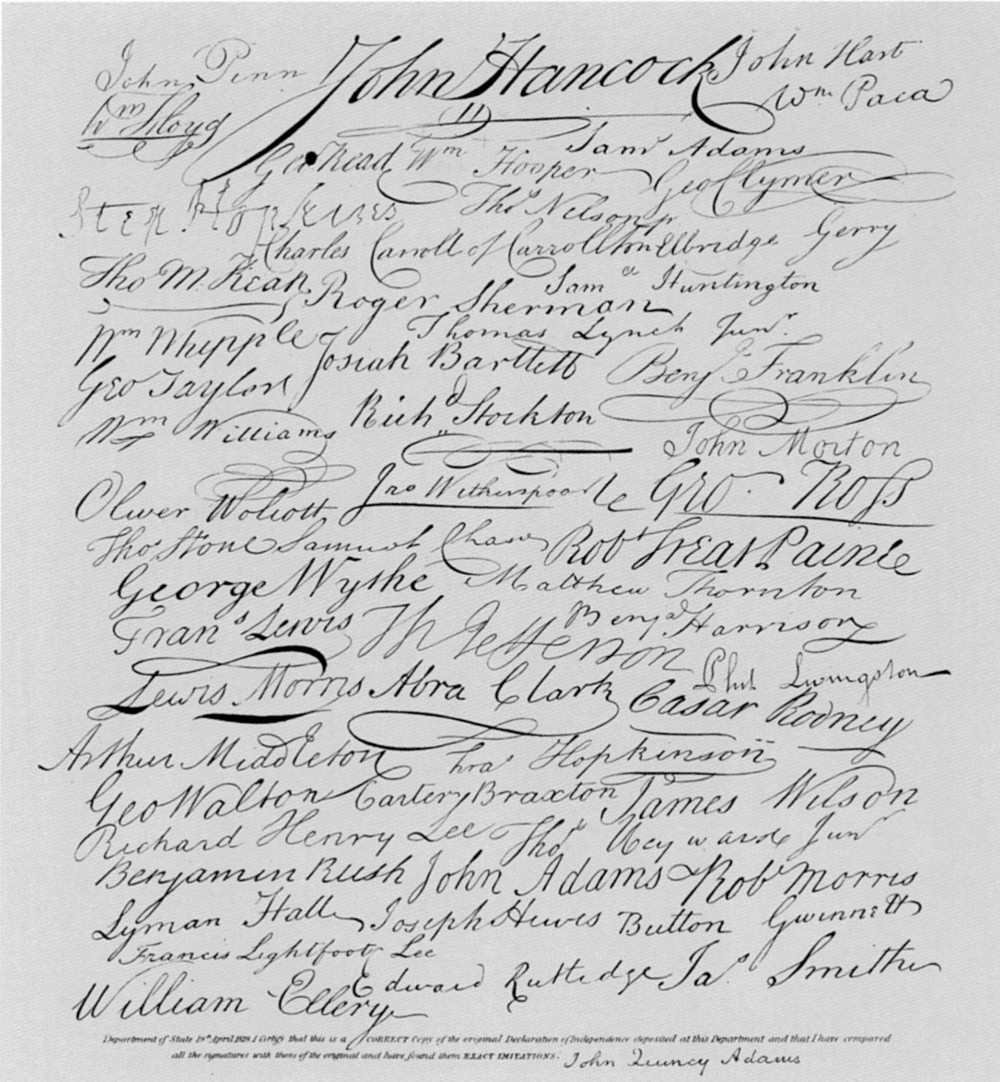

This illustration shows all the signatures on the Declaration of Independence; John Hancock (above) signed first and with the most elegant penmanship.

occurred on August 2. John Hancock, president of the Congress, was the first to sign, and his signature is the boldest. Most of the signers were present on August 2, and the rest later added their autographs. Included among the signers were two future presidents (John Adams and Thomas Jefferson), three vice presidents,

In the days after the Declaration of Independence was signed (above), copies were printed, and it was read to joyous crowds throughout the colonies (opposite page).

sixteen state governors, and ten members of the United States Congress. Signing as part of the Delaware delegation was Caesar Rodney, who died of cancer eight years later. He was suffering from the disease even while making his famous eighty-mile race to Philadelphia. The best British doctors surely could have eased his pain, but Rodney was a rebel who backed independence. He was therefore denied the assistance of British medical experts.

Copies of the Declaration were printed in Philadelphia and sent to cities and villages in all the colonies. Excited crowds gathered at town squares to hear local officials read the document. When the Declaration was read in Philadelphia,

The announcement of the Declaration of Independence touched off celebrations in which American patriots destroyed symbols of Great Britain's rule. Here, people tear down a statue of the king of England.

John Adams reported, "Three cheers rendered. The bells rang all day and almost all night." After a reading in Savannah, Georgia, the townspeople held a mock funeral procession, and symbolically "buried" King George III.

The Declaration of Independence helped to unite what had been a divided land. Pro-British and fence-sitting colonists lost their influence under the power of Jefferson's words. Radicals now became the patriots; the timid were thought of as traitors.

The king's coat of arms is removed from the Philadelphia State House, signifying that England no longer rules the colonies.

After the Revolutionary War ended in 1783, the spirit of the Declaration of Independence marched outward to foreign lands. Just six years later, the people of France rose up against their king, using the American document as their guiding light. In the early 1800s, Latin American countries began breaking away from three centuries of

John Adams

Spanish rule. Leaders of those Latin American revolutions had studied the American Declaration. Probably no single document has had such an impact on the modern world as the one written in 1776 by Thomas Jefferson.

The United States was an established nation in 1826, when John Adams, age ninety-one, lay dying in his house at Quincy, Massachusetts. He struggled to stay alive until July 4 so he could mark one more anniversary of the Declaration, one more birthday of the nation. His last words reflected thoughts of an old friend: "Thomas Jefferson still survives."

Some five hundred miles away, in Monticello, Virginia, eighty-three-year-old Thomas Jefferson was also near death. Shortly after midnight of July 3, 1826, Jefferson asked his granddaughter, who stood at his bedside, "This is the fourth?" She told him it was, and then perhaps he smiled. In one of the most remarkable coincidences in history, Thomas Jefferson and John Adams—the two great architects of the American Revolution—died within hours of each other on July 4, 1826. It was the fiftieth anniversary of the Declaration of Independence.

IN CONGRESS, JULY 4, 1776

The unanimous Declaration of the thirteen united States of America,

When in the Course of human events it becomes necessary for one people to dissolve the political bands which have connected them with another, and to assume among the powers of the earth, the separate and equal station to which the Laws of Nature and of Nature's God entitle them, a decent respect to the opinions of mankind requires that they should declare the causes which impel them to the separation. — We hold these truths to be self-evident, that all men are created equal, that they are endowed by their Creator with certain unalienable Rights, that among these are Life, Liberty and the pursuit of Happiness. — That to secure these rights, Governments are instituted among Men, deriving their just powers from the consent of the governed, — That whenever any Form of Government becomes destructive of these ends, it is the Right of the People to alter or to abolish it, and to institute new Government, laying its foundation on such principles and organizing its powers in such form, as to them shall seem most likely to effect their Safety and Happiness. Prudence, indeed, will dictate that Governments long established should not be changed for light and transient causes; and accordingly all experience hath shewn, that mankind are more disposed to suffer, while evils are sufferable, than to right themselves by abolishing the forms to which they are accustomed. But when a long train of abuses and usurpations, pursuing invariably the same Object evinces a design to reduce them under absolute Despotism, it is their right, it is their duty, to throw off such Government, and to provide new Guards for their future security. — Such has been the patient sufferance of these Colonies; and such is now the necessity which constrains them to alter their former Systems of Government. The history of the present King of Great Britain is a history of repeated injuries and usurpations, all having in direct object the establishment of an absolute Tyranny over these States. To prove this, let Facts be submitted to a candid world. — He has refused his Assent to Laws, the most wholesome and necessary for the public good. — He has forbidden his Governors to pass Laws of immediate and pressing importance, unless suspended in their operation till his Assent should be obtained; and when so suspended, he has utterly neglected to attend to them. — He has refused to pass other Laws for the accommodation of large districts of people, unless those people would relinquish the right of Representation in the Legislature, a right inestimable to them and formidable to tyrants only. — He has called together legislative bodies at places unusual, uncomfortable, and distant from the depository of their public Records, for the sole purpose of fatiguing them into compliance with his measures. — He has dissolved Representative Houses repeatedly, for opposing with manly firmness his invasions on the rights of the people. — He has refused for a long time, after such dissolutions, to cause others to be elected; whereby the Legislative powers, incapable of Annihilation, have returned to the People at large for their exercise; the State remaining in the mean time exposed to all the dangers of invasion from without, and convulsions within. — He has endeavoured to prevent the population of these States; for that purpose obstructing the Laws for Naturalization of Foreigners; refusing to pass others to encourage their migrations hither, and raising the conditions of new Appropriations of Lands. — He has obstructed the Administration of Justice, by refusing his Assent to Laws for establishing Judiciary powers. — He has made Judges dependent on his Will alone, for the tenure of their offices, and the amount and payment of their salaries. — He has erected a multitude of New Offices, and sent hither swarms of Officers to harrass our people, and eat out their substance. — He has kept among us, in times of peace, Standing Armies without the Consent of our legislatures. — He has affected to render the Military independent of and superior to the Civil power. — He has combined with others to subject us to a jurisdiction foreign to our constitution, and unacknowledged by our laws; giving his Assent to their Acts of pretended Legislation: — For Quartering large bodies of armed troops among us: — For protecting them, by a mock Trial, from punishment for any Murders which they should commit on the Inhabitants of these States: — For cutting off our Trade with all parts of the world: — For imposing Taxes on us without our Consent: — For depriving us in many cases, of the benefits of Trial by Jury: — For transporting us beyond Seas to be tried for pretended offences — For abolishing the free System of English Laws in a neighbouring Province, establishing therein an Arbitrary government, and enlarging its Boundaries so as to render it at once an example and fit instrument for introducing the same absolute rule into these Colonies: — For taking away our Charters, abolishing our most valuable Laws, and altering fundamentally the Forms of our Governments: — For suspending our own Legislatures, and declaring themselves invested with power to legislate for us in all cases whatsoever. — He has abdicated Government here, by declaring us out of his Protection and waging War against us. — He has plundered our seas, ravaged our Coasts, burnt our towns, and destroyed the lives of our people. — He is at this time transporting large Armies of foreign Mercenaries to compleat the works of death, desolation and tyranny, already begun with circumstances of Cruelty & perfidy scarcely paralleled in the most barbarous ages, and totally unworthy the Head of a civilized nation. — He has constrained our fellow Citizens taken Captive on the high Seas to bear Arms against their Country, to become the executioners of their friends and Brethren, or to fall themselves by their Hands. — He has excited domestic insurrections amongst us, and has endeavoured to bring on the inhabitants of our frontiers, the merciless Indian Savages, whose known rule of warfare, is an undistinguished destruction of all ages, sexes and conditions. In every stage of these Oppressions We have Petitioned for Redress in the most humble terms: Our repeated Petitions have been answered only by repeated injury. A Prince whose character is thus marked by every act which may define a Tyrant, is unfit to be the ruler of a free people. Nor have We been wanting in attentions to our Brittish brethren. We have warned them from time to time of attempts by their legislature to extend an unwarrantable jurisdiction over us. We have reminded them of the circumstances of our emigration and settlement here. We have appealed to their native justice and magnanimity, and we have conjured them by the ties of our common kindred to disavow these usurpations, which, would inevitably interrupt our connections and correspondence. They too have been deaf to the voice of justice and of consanguinity. We must, therefore, acquiesce in the necessity, which denounces our Separation, and hold them, as we hold the rest of mankind, Enemies in War, in Peace Friends. —

We, therefore, the Representatives of the united States of America, in General Congress, Assembled, appealing to the Supreme Judge of the world for the rectitude of our intentions, do, in the Name, and by Authority of the good People of these Colonies, solemnly publish and declare, That these United Colonies are, and of Right ought to be Free and Independent States; that they are Absolved from all Allegiance to the British Crown, and that all political connection between them and the State of Great Britain, is and ought to be totally dissolved; and that as Free and Independent States, they have full Power to levy War, conclude Peace, contract Alliances, establish Commerce, and to do all other Acts and Things which Independent States may of right do. — And for the support of this Declaration, with a firm reliance on the protection of divine Providence, we mutually pledge to each other our Lives, our Fortunes and our sacred Honor.

John Hancock

Button Gwinnett
Lyman Hall
Geo Walton.

Wm Hooper
Joseph Hewes,
John Penn

Edward Rutledge.

Thos Heyward Junr.
Thomas Lynch Junr.
Arthur Middleton

Samuel Chase
Wm Paca
Thos Stone
Charles Carroll of Carrollton

George Wythe
Richard Henry Lee
Th Jefferson.
Benj Harrison
Thos Nelson jr.
Francis Lightfoot Lee
Carter Braxton

Robt Morris
Benjamin Rush
Benj. Franklin
John Morton
Geo Clymer
Jas. Smith
Geo. Taylor
James Wilson
Geo. Ross

Caesar Rodney
Geo Read
Thos M:Kean

Wm Floyd
Phil. Livingston
Frans. Lewis
Lewis Morris

Richd. Stockton
Jno Witherspoon
Fras. Hopkinson
John Hart
Abra Clark

Josiah Bartlett
Wm Whipple
Saml Adams
John Adams
Robt Treat Paine
Elbridge Gerry
Step. Hopkins
William Ellery
Roger Sherman
Sam el Huntington
Wm Williams
Oliver Wolcott
Matthew Thornton

GLOSSARY

abolish – to outlaw or get rid of

breach – a break; a "breach of law" is an act that goes against a law

colony – a state owned and ruled by another country; the thirteen American colonies were states under the rule of the British government

Continental Congress – gatherings of delegates from the American colonies; the First Continental Congress met in 1774, and the Second Continental Congress met on May 10, 1775 (it eventually adopted the Declaration of Independence)

delegate – a single person who represents a larger group of people

endowed – to be given; Jefferson wrote that people are "endowed by their Creator with certain unalienable rights"—or, God has given people unalienable rights

French and Indian War (1754–1763) – a war between England and France over rights to North American territory in what is now southeastern Canada

grievance – a formal complaint

impel – to urge or push forward

mother country – one's country of origin; for most American colonists, England was their "mother country"

patriot – one who is loyal (or patriotic) to his or her country

quill – an ink pen made from the feather of a bird

rebellion – the attempt to defy, or go against, the authority of a government

reconciliation – an agreement to make peace

self-evident – something that is obvious and needs no proof or explanation; a truth

statute – a law or rule

treason – an act intended to harm one's own government

unalienable (or inalienable) – unable to be denied; a person's "unalienable right" is one that even a government cannot take away

TIMELINE

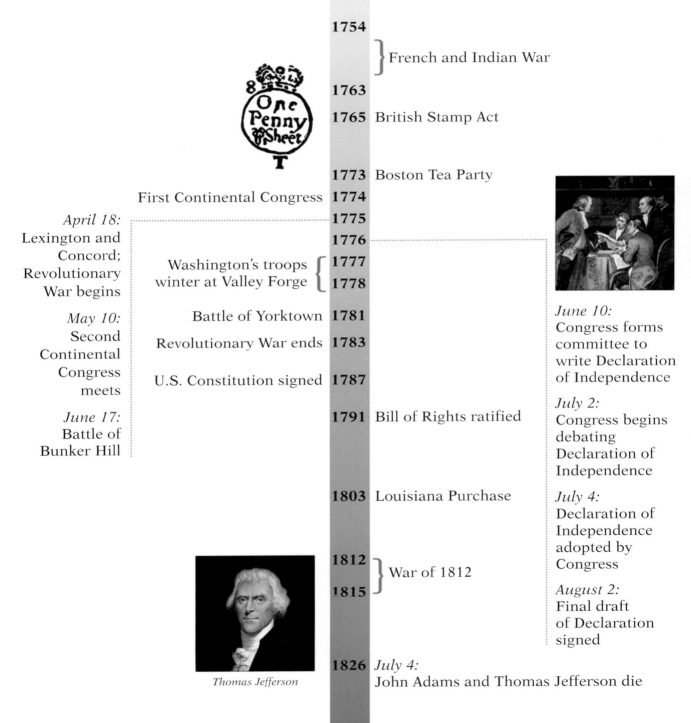

1754–**1763** French and Indian War

1765 British Stamp Act

1773 Boston Tea Party

1774 First Continental Congress

1775

April 18: Lexington and Concord; Revolutionary War begins

May 10: Second Continental Congress meets

June 17: Battle of Bunker Hill

1776

June 10: Congress forms committee to write Declaration of Independence

July 2: Congress begins debating Declaration of Independence

July 4: Declaration of Independence adopted by Congress

August 2: Final draft of Declaration signed

1777–**1778** Washington's troops winter at Valley Forge

1781 Battle of Yorktown

1783 Revolutionary War ends

1787 U.S. Constitution signed

1791 Bill of Rights ratified

1803 Louisiana Purchase

1812–**1815** War of 1812

Thomas Jefferson

1826 *July 4:*
John Adams and Thomas Jefferson die

INDEX (Page numbers in **boldface** type indicate photos or illustrations.)

PHOTO CREDITS

Cover, ©J. L. G. Ferris, Archives of '76, Bay Village, Ohio; 1, Architect of the Capitol; 2, Stock Montage, Inc.; 3, The Bettmann Archive; 4, 5 (top), North Wind Picture Archives; 5 (side), Stock Montage, Inc.; 6, Library of Congress; 7 (both pictures), North Wind Picture Archives; 8, AP/Wide World; 9, Stock Montage, Inc.; 11, AP/Wide World; 12, 14 (both pictures), North Wind Picture Archives; 15 (top), Manuscript Print Collection, Special Collections Department, University of Virginia Library; 15 (bottom), Courtesy Independence National Historical Park; 16, Stock Montage, Inc.; 17, 18, 19, 21, 23 (both pictures), North Wind Picture Archives; 24, Stock Montage, Inc.; 25, 26, 27, 28, 29, North Wind Picture Archives; 30 (bottom left), Courtesy Independence National Historical Park; 30 (top left), 31 (top left, bottom left), Stock Montage, Inc.; 31 (top right), North Wind Picture Archives

Additional Picture Identifications:
Cover: "Drafting the Declaration of Independence, 1776" by J. L. G. Ferris
Page 1: "The Declaration of Independence" by John Trumbull
Page 2: The Declaration of Independence and the Constitution, as they were once displayed at the Library of Congress in Washington, D.C.; both documents have since been moved to the National Archives.
Page 29: The Declaration of Independence

Project Editor: Mark Friedman
Design and Electronic Composition: TJS Design
Photo Editor: Jan Izzo
Cornerstones of Freedom Logo: David Cunningham

ABOUT THE AUTHOR

R. Conrad Stein was born and grew up in Chicago. After serving in the U.S. Marine Corps, he attended the University of Illinois, where he earned a B.A. in history. He later studied in Mexico, where he received an advanced degree in fine arts.

Reading history is Mr. Stein's hobby. He tries to bring the excitement of history to his work. Mr. Stein has published many history books aimed at young readers. He lives in Chicago with his wife and their daughter Janna.